Color, Draw, Collage

Color, Draw, Collage

CREATE YOUR WAY TO A LESS STRESSFUL LIFE!

Jill Howell

Skyhorse Publishing

Skyhorse Publishing books may be purchased in bulk at special discounts for sales promotion, corporate gifts, fund-raising, or educational purposes. Special editions can also be created to specifications. For details, contact the Special Sales Department, Skyhorse Publishing, 307 West 36th Street, 11th Floor, New York, NY 10018 or info@skyhorsepublishing.com.

Skyhorse® and Skyhorse Publishing® are registered trademarks of Skyhorse Publishing, Inc.®, a Delaware corporation.

Visit our website at www.skyhorsepublishing.com.

10 9 8 7 6 5 4 3

Library of Congress Cataloging-in-Publication Data

Names: Howell, Jill, author.
Title: Color, draw, collage : create your way to a less stressful life! / Jill Howell.
Description: New York, NY : Skyhorse Publishing, [2017]
Identifiers: LCCN 2016054120 | ISBN 9781510717244 (paperback)
Subjects: LCSH: Art therapy. | Self-care, Health. | BISAC: SELF-HELP / Creativity.
Classification: LCC RC489.A7 H69 2017 | DDC 616.89/1656--dc23 LC record available at https://lccn.loc.gov/2016054120
Cover design by Jane Sheppard
Cover illustration by Jill Howell

ISBN: 978-1-5107-1724-4

Printed in the United States of America

This book is dedicated to my patients. You inspire, amaze, and teach me how to be a better therapist and a better human being. Thank you.

What is this book?

This is a workbook designed to teach you how to deal with the stressors of every day in a creative way! This book is not an answer to all your problems, but it will guide you to learn new ways to help yourself when you are experiencing stress. It will also help you to maintain lower levels of stress so you are better equipped to deal with life's big stressors. Just purchasing this workbook is a big step! It means that you know that you need some help and that you are willing to do the work toward better self-care.

If you should experience overwhelming emotions that are difficult for you to deal with while using this guide, please contact a psychiatric professional. If you don't already have a counselor, you can call your insurance company, employer, or county mental health services. You can also call an Art Therapist!

What is an Art Therapist?

An Art Therapist is a graduate-level psychiatric professional who has been trained to use art as a tool for counseling. Art therapists can be Registered (ATR) and Board Certified (BC). To find an Art Therapist in your area, go to arttherapy.org

Who am I?

I am a Registered, Board Certified Art Therapist and a Licensed Professional Counselor (LPC). I work at a hospital and a cancer center to help patients deal with the stress of being sick.

This is me!

But I can't even draw a straight line!

Art Therapists hear that a lot! That's okay, I don't want you to! There is NO judgment here! I mean that. This is just for you. You don't have to share it, and no one ever has to see it if you don't want them to. Art Therapy is not about making great art. It can be, but that is not what is important. What's important is that you use the art as a means to help you to learn more about yourself. This book is more about art as therapy. Making art is fun! It is a great release of stress. This workbook is designed to help you learn coping skills while having fun and destressing at the same time. You can use stick figures or even just colors, shapes, lines, or symbols to represent how you are feeling.

What you will need

You can't make art without supplies. Gather colored pencils, magic markers, oil pastels, or even crayons. You will also need some old magazines and a glue stick and scissors for collages. Collage is simply tearing out or cutting up images and arranging them on the page. It's really fun, and you probably haven't done it since kindergarten!

Let's get started!

What is Stress?

Merriam-Webster defines stress as a factor that induces bodily or mental tension. Yuck!

We all have some stress in our lives, some more than others and some more often. Stress can be a good thing; it can motivate us to get a job done or to do our best. Stress is not a problem when it happens once in a while. It is, however, a problem when it happens a lot!

What would you do? Draw yourself reacting to this situation.

Why is it a problem?

Stress does bad things to our body. Have you heard of the expression "fight or flight," or sometimes even "freeze"? When faced with immediate danger, our bodies prepare to fight or flee, and the blood rushes to our arms and legs so we can run or fight. We don't need to use our digestive system or our immune system to run, so those systems turn off. After the danger is resolved, the body will begin to calm itself, and all systems will return to functioning fully. Unfortunately, we are often stressed for a prolonged period of time, clogging up our digestion and inhibiting our immune system; imagine what havoc is being wreaked on our bodies!

You can't take care of it if you are not aware of it!

The most important thing about dealing with stress is awareness. Pay attention to the signs that your body is giving you. Our bodies are very aware of our stressors. You may feel butterflies in your stomach, or sweaty palms . . .

Draw on this body the physical signs of stress that you feel. Use color, lines, and shapes. Don't hold back, this shouldn't be pretty!

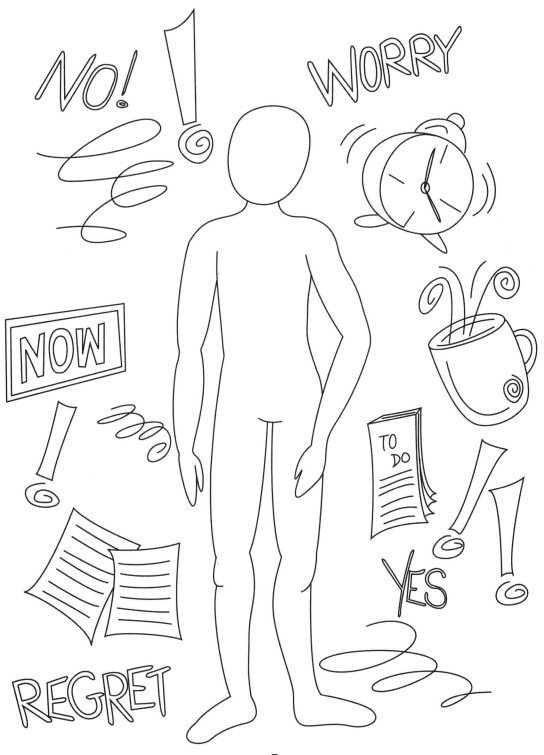

The more you pay attention to your body and the signs it is giving you, the quicker you can identify and stop the triggers that are causing you the stress.

To become more aware of your stress level, imagine that you have a bucket. All day you are putting emotions into that bucket. Things that annoyed you, upset you, made you feel frustrated or sad or angry. The bucket keeps getting more and more full throughout your day, unless you stop it. Then, you get a phone call, a new project at work, someone that you love is sick or injured, something didn't go as planned . . . what happens to your bucket? You guessed it! It overflows.

When your bucket overflows, that is when your body will begin showing signs of illness. I am sure that you have experienced that moment when you were under a lot of pressure and then, you sneeze! Oh no! On top of *all of this* I have a cold!! Yup, there goes the immune system. It's been running on low for too long.

Use symbols or collage or words to fill the bucket with your stressors.

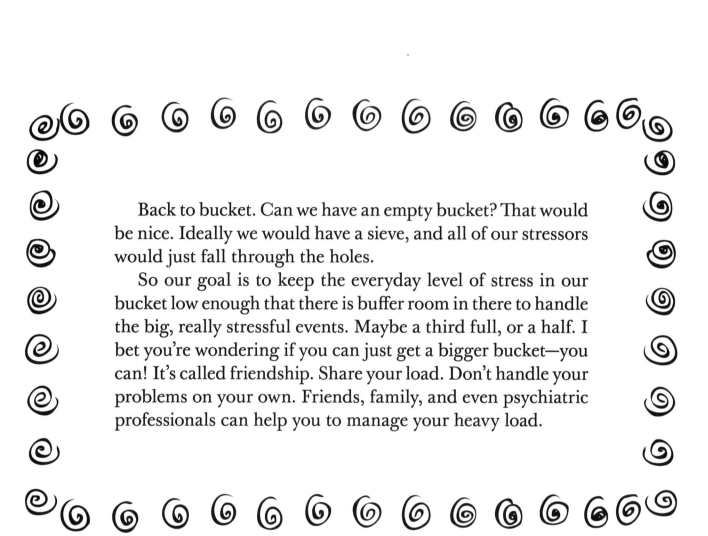

Back to bucket. Can we have an empty bucket? That would be nice. Ideally we would have a sieve, and all of our stressors would just fall through the holes.

So our goal is to keep the everyday level of stress in our bucket low enough that there is buffer room in there to handle the big, really stressful events. Maybe a third full, or a half. I bet you're wondering if you can just get a bigger bucket—you can! It's called friendship. Share your load. Don't handle your problems on your own. Friends, family, and even psychiatric professionals can help you to manage your heavy load.

Draw pictures of you and your BFF, family member, or support person doing something fun. If you don't have one now, either draw your ideal support person or remember someone from your childhood.

Sometimes we are really at our wit's end. This is why it is so important to create buffer space in your bucket. If you can manage to keep your daily stressors down to a minimum, then you will be able to handle the big events. If you are walking around saying, "I can't take one more thing!" then you will be too overwhelmed to handle the one more thing that will eventually come your way. So check in with your bucket daily. Evaluate how full it is.

Draw a selfie of you at your wit's end. Really be expressive here, and remember, this is NOT about making pretty art!

Selfie

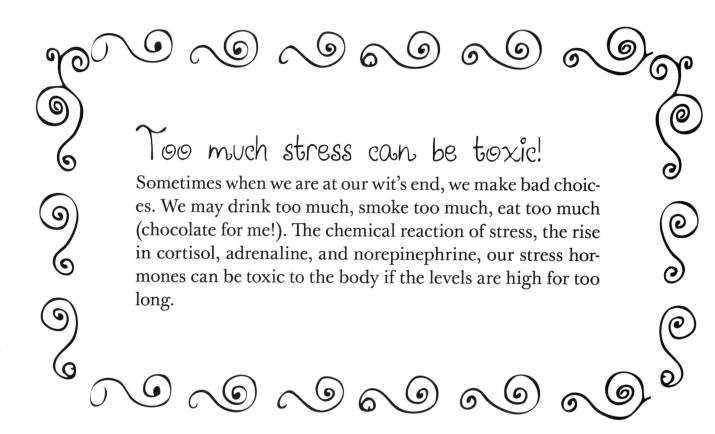

Too much stress can be toxic!

Sometimes when we are at our wit's end, we make bad choices. We may drink too much, smoke too much, eat too much (chocolate for me!). The chemical reaction of stress, the rise in cortisol, adrenaline, and norepinephrine, our stress hormones can be toxic to the body if the levels are high for too long.

Collage or draw the toxic activities that you do you do when you are stressed.

Ahhhhh, this will make me feel better!

If your bucket is getting too full, then you need to do something with the intention of reducing it. You can just go about doing things that you like to do, and you may feel a bit better. However, if you supercharge your activities with the intention to reduce your stress, that intention can become a magical power!

For example, say that you have checked in with your bucket and it's starting to get up there, and you realize, "Wow, this is REALLY a stressful day!" Say to yourself, "I can't wait till I _____." I can't wait to go to my yoga class, walk my dog, watch my favorite television show . . . You can do whatever activity that you love and not really think much about it, or you can have your mind tell your body what it needs to do (release your stress) and how it is going to do it (take a walk). When you set the intention for your mind and your body to work together, every activity that you do becomes a powerful tool for stress management.

So, it's not that you are necessarily doing different activities, but that you are *thinking* about your activities differently. Get yourself psyched up to do something that you know will help you to feel better. When you feel stressed, look forward to a fun activity; think about it, plan for it.

In your calendar write in your weekly self-care activities that you most look forward to. Include meals with friends, a bubble bath, an exercise class, favorite TV shows . . . If your calendar is too empty, schedule in some new activities that are just for you; even half an hour will help.

Shake it Off!

Stress affects us physically, and we know that it sticks to us in all sorts of places: muscles, bones, organs, our energy. Stress is like cooties! Do you remember running from cooties when you were a child? You would get a cootie shot and shake off your whole body to release the cooties.

Color the cooties and draw some more. What do cooties look like to you?

Color in the places where stress has caused lasting effects on your body. Go ahead, label all of your physical complaints; it is part of releasing them. Make sure to include the places on your body where stress likes to settle. Do you get an upset stomach? Difficulty breathing? Sore shoulders?

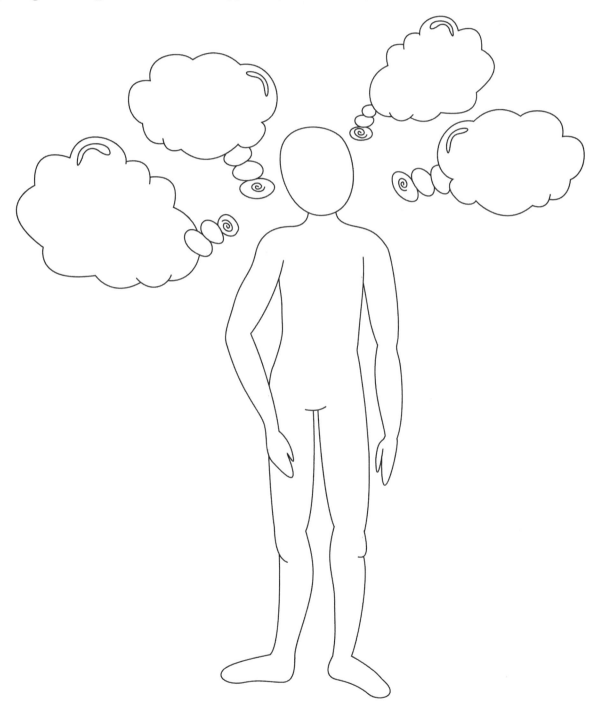

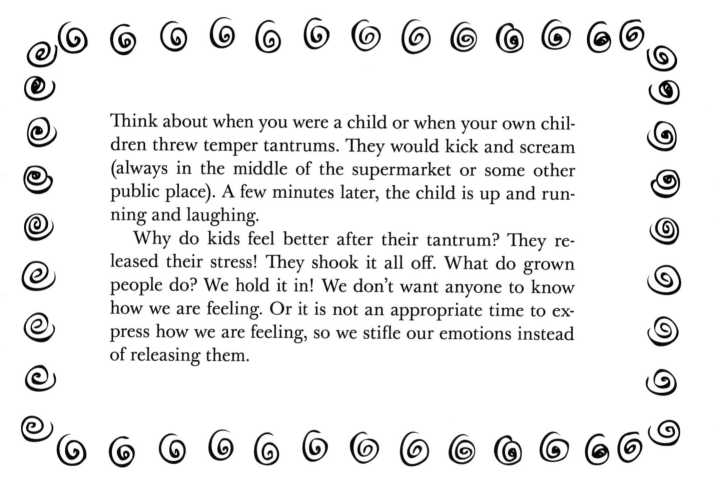

Think about when you were a child or when your own children threw temper tantrums. They would kick and scream (always in the middle of the supermarket or some other public place). A few minutes later, the child is up and running and laughing.

Why do kids feel better after their tantrum? They released their stress! They shook it all off. What do grown people do? We hold it in! We don't want anyone to know how we are feeling. Or it is not an appropriate time to express how we are feeling, so we stifle our emotions instead of releasing them.

We all have the urge at times to just let go and release our wrath. Draw a picture of yourself having a wild temper tantrum or journal about what it might feel like.

Fill the body with words or images that describe what you hold inside of you in order to not release your feelings (sometimes we even stuff potato chips in there).

Throwing a temper tantrum is not the best solution for grown-ups. It raises your blood pressure and sends your body's systems into chaos. We need to find a way to physically release our stress, to literally *shake it off*! Dance around your living room. Don't look for the best parking spot—find one in the back of the lot and walk. Take a flight of stairs instead of the escalator. Go for a walk. Try an exercise class. The more physical activity you get, the less stressed you will feel. Do whatever you can within your own physical ability. There is NO excuse not to move. Can't get up? Dance in your chair!

Here is a wonderful way to brush off stress. It only takes a minute—everyone has at least one minute.

Starting at the top of your head, use your palms to brush off any negative thoughts or feelings. Brush down your shoulders and your arms. Brush under your arms. Brush off the front of your torso, down the sides of your torso, and your back. Continue brushing down the front, sides, and back of your legs. While you do this, imagine that you are brushing off your stress and any negative energy that is surrounding you. Wiggle a little, maybe jump up and down some. Now take a deep breath and release!

Label the arrows with whatever stressors you are brushing off your body.

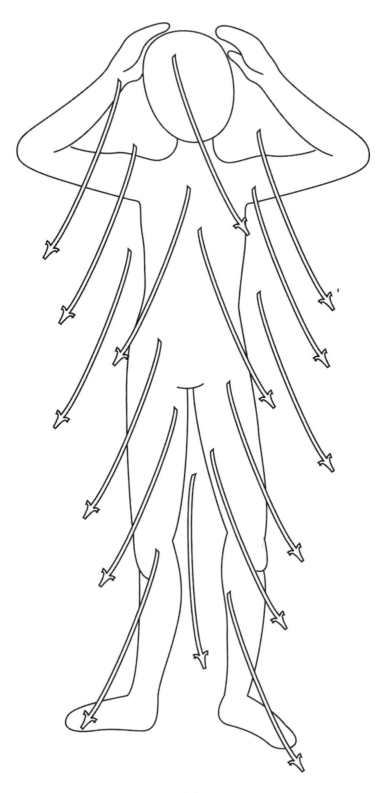

Go through magazines and cut out images of physical activities that you would like to do. You can do it here or on a separate piece of paper that you can hang on your refrigerator to remind you to get moving!

Dear Diary,

Another great physical release is writing. Sometimes we have all sorts of non-sense built up and spinning around in our heads. Writing is an excellent way to stop ruminating. Ruminating is when we just can't stop thinking about the same thing over and over. If you have thoughts that are particularly bother-some and may be keeping you up at night or preventing you from being your best self for a prolonged period of time, then it would be best to speak with a counselor or clergy.

When we write, we can imagine physically taking the thoughts out of our heads and sending them down the arm and out our hands onto the paper. One of my favorite stress management techniques is to *write and rip!* Instead of writing in a diary that you will keep forever, you write in a spiral notebook, then tear out the paper and rip it into tiny little pieces! The ripping feels great. When you know that you are going to rip it up immediately, then you don't need to worry about editing your thoughts or worry about your spell-ing, handwriting, or language!

If you are feeling really angry at someone, instead of confronting them, write it out first. Go ahead, be nasty, no one will ever read it. Release your anger on to the paper. Will this solve all of your problems? No, of course not. But how clearly are you thinking when your emotions are all worked up?

Think of the writing as a steam valve, a release for some of your emotions. You will be thinking a lot more clearly if you can blow off some of that steam onto the paper. If you are feeling calm, then you will be able communicate your thoughts more clearly to the person you are disagreeing with. If you are not feeling any better, try doing the exercise additional times!

Writing is also helpful when we are feeling sad or alone. It's an excellent tool for grieving—write to the person you're missing. On the next page, write back to yourself imagining what this person would say to help you feel better.

Using a separate piece of paper, take a few minutes to write about some-thing that is stressing you. When you are done, tear it up into tiny pieces! Turn the pieces so that the writing is facing down and rearrange them into an image or a fun abstract visual. Glue them down so no one can read it!

Take your emotional temperature now. Are you feeling any better? Cooler? Lighter? Color in the thermometers to represent how you are feeling.

What did you say? I wasn't listening.

Have you ever been so absorbed in activity that time seemed to just fly by? When we can distract our thoughts away from what is bothering us and focus on something else, we just simply feel better. As the mind focuses on something enjoyable, the body triggers the relaxation response, the opposite of the stress reaction. Everything slows down, muscles release, organs function properly. We WANT to feel this way! Our bodies like to feel happy and healthy.

What are some activities that you do that absorb your mind, even if just for a short period of time?

Use three different color markers to color the activities that you do all of the time, only sometimes, and the ones that you would like to do more often. Add some of your own ideas!

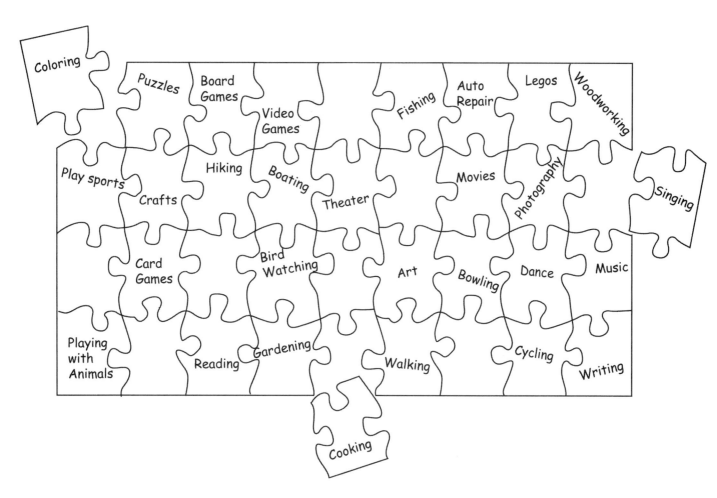

If you are having a hard time with this, think about the activities that you enjoyed doing as a child.

Draw a picture of yourself as a kid doing something that you used to love to do. Would you like to do this activity now? Why aren't you?

Me, as a kid!

In the moment

It is important to have some quick and easy distractions available for you to use in the moment that you are feeling stressed. This is when many people choose to smoke or eat or pick up other unhealthy habits! If you have 2–3 healthy quick fixes in your bag of tricks, then you are much more likely to make a better choice in that stressful moment.

Smartphones provide many options for a quick distraction. Check in with a friend, play a quick game, listen to a meditation (more about that later on page 52).

The best in-the-moment distraction that we have is something that you have probably heard so often that you don't even think about. Stop whatever it is that you are doing or thinking about and BREATHE! You can train your body that the breath is a signal for relaxation. It is not that important *how* you breathe. What is important is that you are stopping and *focusing* on your breath. This really works well, if you take the time and make the commitment to practice.

Begin when you aren't stressed; use the spare moments throughout your day. In line at the supermarket, stopped at a red light, waiting for an elevator, going to the bathroom . . . and turn your focus to your breath. It may help to identify repetitive moments in your day, perhaps every time that you check your email, or when you finish a phone call or complete a task.

Monkey Brain

It is difficult to stay focused on just the breath when you aren't used to it. Your brain will wander to a million places. You could have 100 distracting thoughts in 30 seconds. The key is to not allow your brain to follow the thoughts and to not get frustrated with yourself. For example, if you are focusing on your breathing and you begin to wonder, *what am I going to make for dinner tonight?*, you can either think about your favorite recipe, and what you don't have in the pantry, and what else you might need from the grocery store. Or you can say to yourself, *Not right now! Right now I am breathing*, and then return your focus to your breath.

Every time you return your focus back inward, that is mindfulness, or simple meditation. These are some of the best techniques you can use to relax the mind and body. Mindfulness is actually paying attention to one thing at a time. Being mindful of brushing your teeth or washing the dishes, without thinking about everything else that you need to do or did that day. This takes practice, but it really does help to relax your body. Over time, you may notice that it is easier for you stay focused and concentrate on the task at hand. Scientists have used MRIs and EEGs to prove that meditation can change brain function, using more of, and enhancing connections in, certain areas of the brain.

Stop for 30 seconds, and count the thoughts that pop into your brain! Fill this brain with words and images of your distracting thoughts.

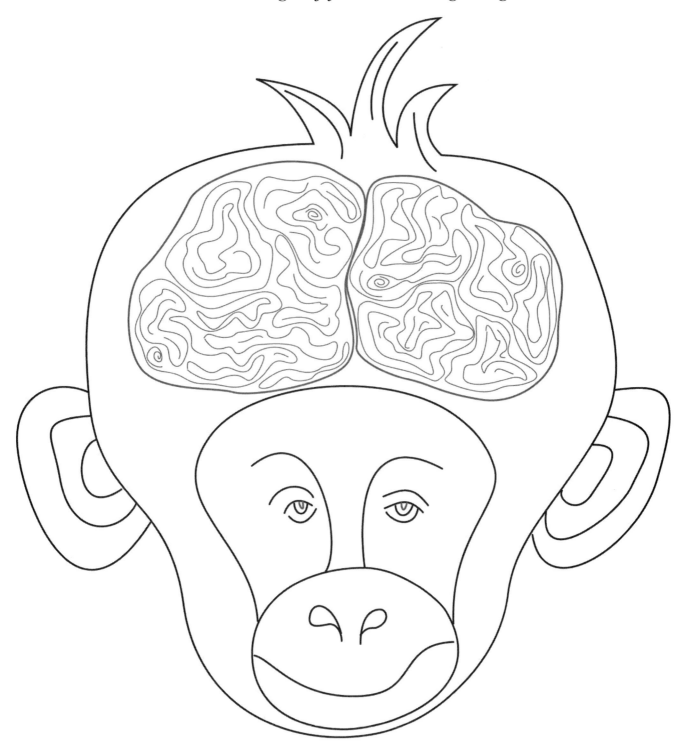

Create an image that will remind you to send those distracting thoughts away. Release the thoughts into puffy clouds, send them down a river, say to yourself, not now. What will you say or visualize to help you to return your focus inward?

How to breathe

It really doesn't matter how you breathe, whether you breathe in through your nose and out through your mouth, or vice versa. What really matters is that you are paying attention to your breath and not to your thoughts. That said, here are some useful breathing techniques to try. Use whatever feels best for you.

When you are breathing to relax yourself, you should always make sure that your feet are grounded on the floor. You can be sitting or standing, but don't cross your legs, since that will make it difficult for the energy from your body and the earth to connect.

The simplest technique is "smell the roses"—breathe in through your nose—and "blow out the candles"—exhale slowly through your mouth.

Draw a picture or collage some images of flowers here. Include your favorite candles or birthday cake, too!

Square breathing is another easy way to watch your breath.

Imagine a square in front of you or use your fingers to draw a square. Breathe up the left side, out as you follow the top, in as you go down the right side, and out as you follow the bottom. Depending on your lungs, you can use a count of two or three along each side of the square. Or try breathing up the left side for a count of three, holding your breath along the top for a count of three, exhaling down the right side for a count of three, and then waiting to inhale the next breath for a count of three. As your breathing and concentration improve, you can increase the count.

My favorite is diaphragmatic breathing, or belly breathing. It is the same kind of breath that singers use—it's very different from the way we normally breathe, and since it is different, it requires more focus. When we are focusing, that is a better distraction. The more that you are focused on the breath, the less you can focus on what is troubling you.

Put your palms on your stomach. Imagine that you have a balloon inside your belly. When you inhale, you are going to inflate the balloon. This is the hardest part because we are used to sucking our bellies in when we breathe. Don't get frustrated, this takes practice. Try to picture the air going into the balloon. You can breathe through either your nose or your mouth. When you exhale, you are going to squeeze the air out of the balloon to deflate it. Use your stomach muscles to squeeze all of the air out. This will also help you to develop a nice six-pack abdomen! Try this a few times, inflate and deflate.

Next, you will inflate the belly and then take in a bit more air in the middle of your chest, under your ribs. Then you can breathe in more deeply and take a full breath into your lungs. Hold it a moment. When you are ready, begin to exhale, first from your upper lungs, your lower lungs, and then squeeze out your belly.

As you do this, you can count—breathe in one to the belly, two to the lower chest, three to the top of your chest, hold, hold, then release three, two, one the opposite way.

Most important, when you breathe in, think *relax, peace, calm, chill*. I say "chill, Jill!" When you breathe out, imagine that you are blowing away whatever or whoever is upsetting you!

Alternate nostril breathing is another technique that requires a lot of focus.

When you first try this, you will want to place a finger on your nostril, but as you learn it better you will be able to do it just by focusing.

Place your finger on your right nostril and inhale through your left. Release your finger and exhale through your right nostril. Place your finger on your left nostril and inhale through your right. Release and exhale from your left. Count as you do this—inhale 1, exhale 1, inhale 2, exhale 2—and when you get to every fifth breath, inhale through both nostrils. If you forget or mess up the count, return to 1 and start again.

Draw an image or write about whomever or whatever you are blowing away.

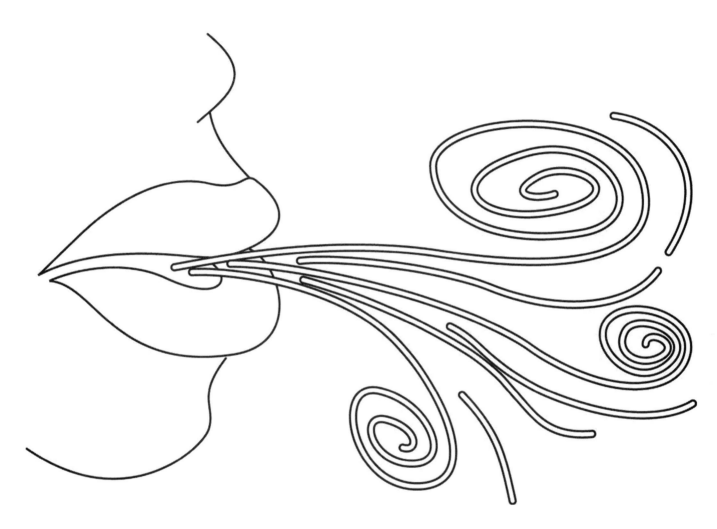

Not now, I am in Maui.

Do you ever just daydream, imagining that you are somewhere else? Well, that can also be called *visualization*, and that is a very powerful tool for relaxation.

Pick one spot, it could be a place where you have been, a place where you have seen in a movie, or anywhere you'd like to go. Think of a favorite vacation spot, the beach, the woods, fishing, your grandmother's living room. Imagine a place that makes you smile and feel calm and safe. Now, memorize it. Really think about the details. If it is outside, what is the season, the temperature? What is the sun doing? The wind? Are you sitting, standing, walking? What are you touching? Really imagine that you are there. What do you smell? Hear? Give this some time and give yourself enough details so that the mind can believe that it is actually there. When the mind thinks that you are in this safe place, it will send the signal to the body to relax. The body does not know that it is not in this imagined place, so the parasympathetic nervous system, the relaxation response, will kick in. All systems will slow down to a healthier pace.

It is best to always use the same spot for your visualization because the mind will remember what it has imagined before and quickly bring your body back to a relaxed state.

My spot is a waterfall. Sometimes I can take two breaths and imagine that I am sitting in front of the waterfall, and I can feel the stress fall off of me. Other times, it's not so easy. Those times, I have to imagine getting into my car, driving to the trail, visualize the entire trail to the waterfall, and then I am ready to picture myself sitting there. So, really put a lot of effort into the details so you will have time to visualize everything and to relax your body.

Color in your happy place!

Pesky thoughts will pop into your mind, of course. Again, don't focus on them. Send them off in the clouds or just say, "Not now. I am in Maui!"

Grab your magazines, especially travel magazines (which make a great daydreaming tool), and cut out images of places that might make good relaxation daydreams for you.

Go outside. Be outside. Feel the outside.

It is easier to visualize nature after spending time in it. Memorize how it feels when you look at a tree, a stream, the ocean. Connecting with nature is important for our health. We need to feel a connection with other living things—even tending to a houseplant can create a calming connection. Treat yourself to those beautiful cut flowers at the grocery store, or plant a garden. Take at least a few minutes daily to connect with and appreciate nature.

Draw your visualization spot here or take a photo and paste it in!

If you had a happy childhood home, a fun exercise is to draw a floor plan or a representation of your house. Imagine yourself walking through the front door and going into all of the rooms, especially your old room. Please do not do this by yourself if it may upset you—save this exercise to do with a trusted friend, family member, or your art therapist or counselor!

Me, the Tree

One of my favorite quick-fix visualizations is to stand in a sunny window or outside in the sun (you can still do it if it's not sunny. I am solar-powered so the actual sun is helpful to me!). Plant both feet firmly on the ground and bend your knees slightly. Imagine that you are a tree. Visualize your roots going down into the ground. If you are inside, perhaps in an office, picture those roots traveling down through each of the floors of the building, down through the basement, and then into the earth. Imagine your roots grounding into the earth, down into the core of the earth. Now picture the core of our earth, think about the heat and the colors, think about all of the energy that is in there. Grab that energy with your roots and suck the energy in and back up. See the reverse of before—go through the earth, the basement, the floors, and back to your feet. See the energy as a color or as light and picture that energy coming up through your feet and into your legs. Bring the energy up your body, into your core, your chest, your head.

Remember that you are a tree; gently stretch your arms up to the sky. Imagine your branches reaching for the sun. Take the energy from the sun, again use color or light to imagine the energy entering your hands. Feel that energy coming down onto the top of your head and bring it into your body. Breathe it into your chest and your core and down to your legs.

This exercise can be done in a matter of minutes and in any public place. No one will know what you are doing, they will just assume that you are stretching, they won't see a large maple tree growing in your cubicle!

Draw yourself as a tree, or paste pictures of your favorite trees here.

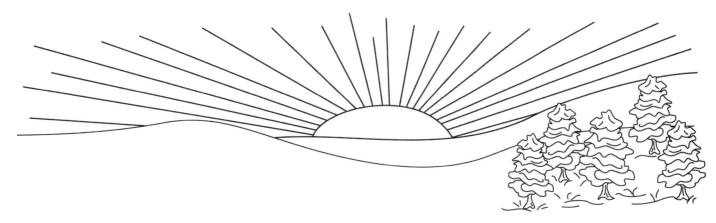

From Ouch to Om

Pain and discomfort can cause extra stress. Visualization can be used to help reduce the intensity of pain. If your pain is overwhelming and affecting your ability to function, it is important to seek medical advice.

Think about your pain. Is it Hot? Cold? Hard? Dull? Try to come up with an image that represents your pain. A knife, a brick, and elephant sitting on you . . . or just use shapes and line and color to represent your pain.

Draw it here. It is best to use the oil pastels for this. After you create your image, think about the opposite, something cool or soft, and draw over your image. Use lighter colors to blend and soften your pain away.

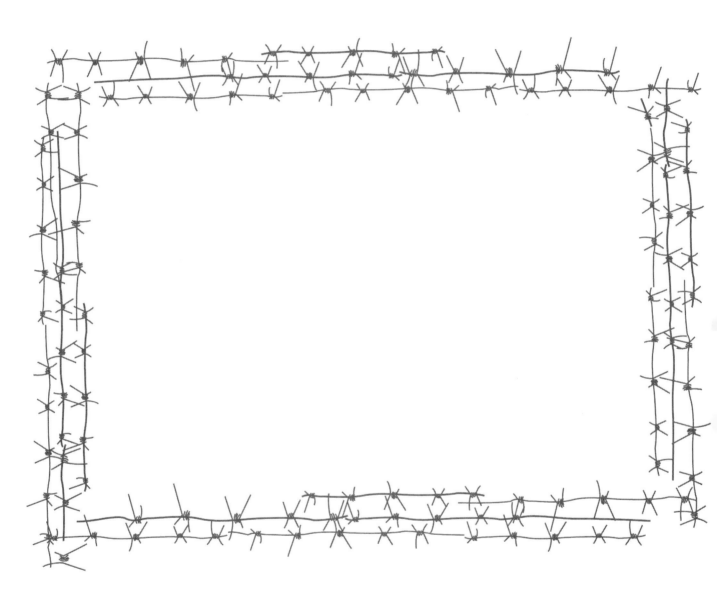

You may want to share this image with your medical professionals and family so they may gain some insight about how you are feeling. It always helps to have a visual aid. If focusing on your pain is disturbing or overwhelming, please talk about it with a psychiatric professional.

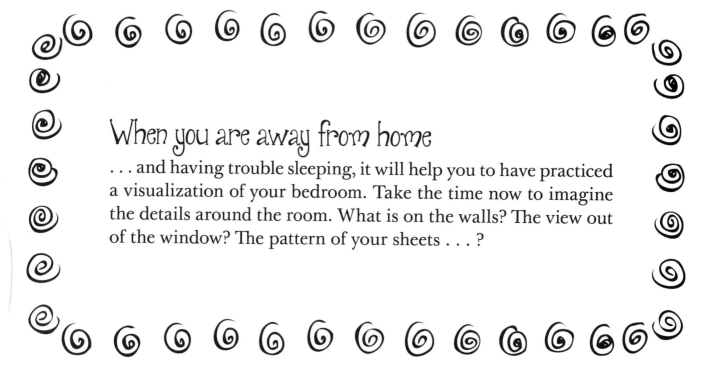

When you are away from home

. . . and having trouble sleeping, it will help you to have practiced a visualization of your bedroom. Take the time now to imagine the details around the room. What is on the walls? The view out of the window? The pattern of your sheets . . . ?

Draw your favorite place to sleep or nap.

Help! I can't stop my brain!

Sometimes we just can't shut the extra voice in our head off. You have tried to tell the voice to go away, sent the thoughts off in a cloud, refocused on feeling like you are in Maui, and yet, there it is—the nagging, stressful voice. Guided imagery (sometimes called guided meditation or guided visualization) can really help to quiet that voice.

Guided imagery is when you listen to a recorded voice guiding you through relaxation techniques. Guided imagery is really helpful because instead of listening to your own voice in your head, your mind is filled with the recorded voice. You are too busy listening to that voice to focus on your own inner voice. The mind is also filled with following directions. The recording will guide you through breathing exercises, imagining beautiful locations, and relaxing different muscles. There are a variety of visualizations for anxiety, pain, stress, insomnia, fear. You can purchase guided imagery CDs on the Internet or you can download an assortment of apps to your phone or tablet. You might want to try a few different ones to find a voice that is the most pleasing to you. Recorded visualizations can range from five minutes to a full hour.

If you need a midday refresher but don't have time for a nap, find a quiet spot and set the intention that you will feel revived and awake. Listening to a guided imagery for five or ten minutes is like pressing a restart button on your day. Quieting your mind will help to clear it and reset it so you will be better equipped to move on.

Never, ever, *ever* listen to guided imagery while you are driving! You must be in a safe, quiet place where you will not be interrupted.

Imagine yourself listening to a relaxing meditation.

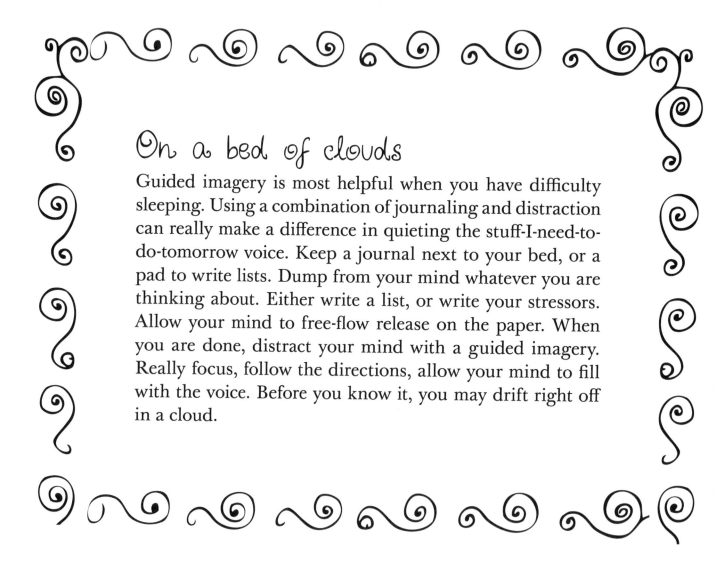

On a bed of clouds

Guided imagery is most helpful when you have difficulty sleeping. Using a combination of journaling and distraction can really make a difference in quieting the stuff-I-need-to-do-tomorrow voice. Keep a journal next to your bed, or a pad to write lists. Dump from your mind whatever you are thinking about. Either write a list, or write your stressors. Allow your mind to free-flow release on the paper. When you are done, distract your mind with a guided imagery. Really focus, follow the directions, allow your mind to fill with the voice. Before you know it, you may drift right off in a cloud.

Imagine a perfect place to sleep, on a cloud, on the beach, on a bed in the woods . . . draw it here or collage images of beds and beautiful places.

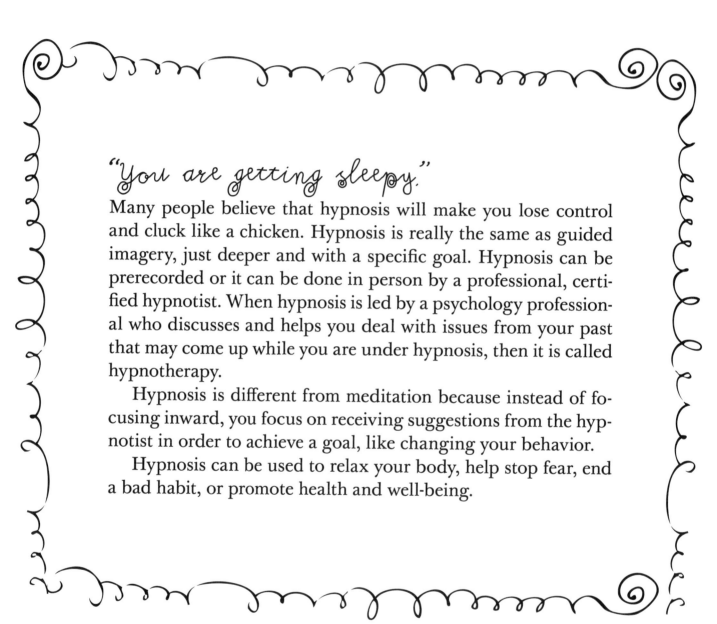

"You are getting sleepy."

Many people believe that hypnosis will make you lose control and cluck like a chicken. Hypnosis is really the same as guided imagery, just deeper and with a specific goal. Hypnosis can be prerecorded or it can be done in person by a professional, certified hypnotist. When hypnosis is led by a psychology professional who discusses and helps you deal with issues from your past that may come up while you are under hypnosis, then it is called hypnotherapy.

Hypnosis is different from meditation because instead of focusing inward, you focus on receiving suggestions from the hypnotist in order to achieve a goal, like changing your behavior.

Hypnosis can be used to relax your body, help stop fear, end a bad habit, or promote health and well-being.

Fill in the thought bubble with a goal that you would like to achieve if you tried hypnosis.

I can't sleep!

No one can face the day without a good night's sleep. Sure, once in a while we stay out late, have too much caffeine, or we just can't stop our brain. Sleep gives the brain the opportunity to sort through the day's activities. The argument with your spouse, the awkward moment with a colleague, the laughter from the lunch with your best friend. The brain decides what is important and what lessons there are to be learned. When the brain relives the activities of the day, many of the thoughts that seemed overwhelming while you were awake will dilute and neutralize overnight. That is why people always say to "sleep on it": you will have a better perspective in the morning. If you are having difficulty sleeping on a regular basis, please consult a health care professional to rule out any medical issues. Otherwise, a sleepless night is a great opportunity to apply the techniques to stop rumination. Whether you have difficulty falling asleep or your snoring partner wakes you up in the middle of the night, this is the best time to utilize stress management tools.

Keep a notebook by your bed. Sometimes it can be a simple thought that is keeping you up: "What if I forget to_____"? If you have a notebook handy, then you can jot down your thoughts and settle your brain. If your mind is really racing, allow yourself ten minutes to journal, then close the book and put it away. It will be there in the morning. Next, apply your relaxation tools. Starting with visualization. Go to your safe place; remember the image that you created on page 44. Go there, really feel like you are there. In that place, imagine thinking about relaxing each of your body parts. Start with your toes and work your way up. Work your way back down if you are still awake. I am getting sleepy just thinking about doing this! If you are having distracting thoughts, remember that that is okay—be kind to yourself and gently bring your mind back to your safe place.

Still having trouble? Use recorded guided imagery or self-hypnosis. Having a voice to focus on will help you concentrate.

Draw a picture on the bedding of a thought or an activity that has been jumbled up into a dream. Go ahead, this is a safe place for all of those wild images that your brain has conjured up. It may feel silly, but these images are helping your brain to process your thoughts. If the images are disturbing, soften them by coloring on top of the image, neutralizing the image like your brain does during sleep.

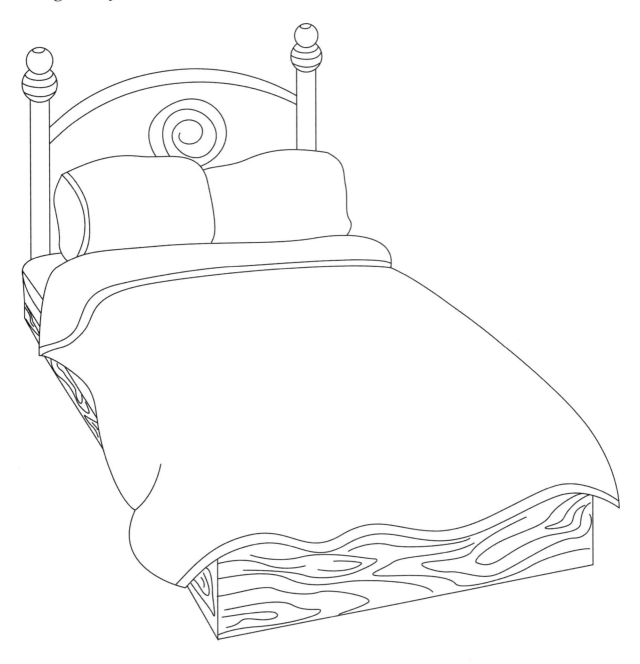

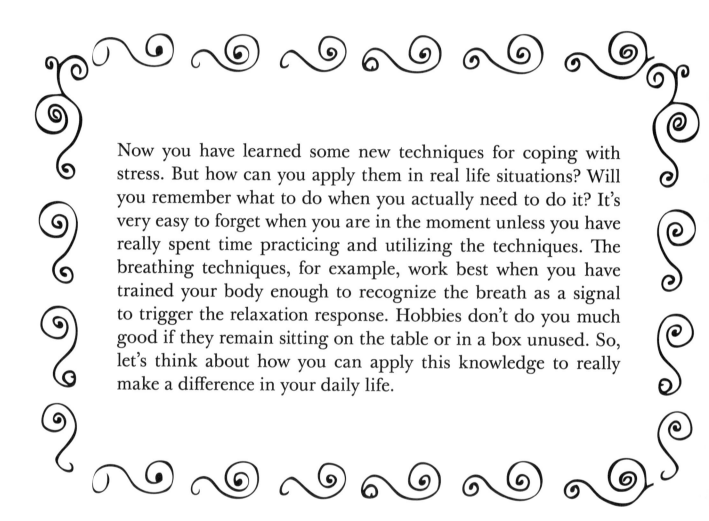

Now you have learned some new techniques for coping with stress. But how can you apply them in real life situations? Will you remember what to do when you actually need to do it? It's very easy to forget when you are in the moment unless you have really spent time practicing and utilizing the techniques. The breathing techniques, for example, work best when you have trained your body enough to recognize the breath as a signal to trigger the relaxation response. Hobbies don't do you much good if they remain sitting on the table or in a box unused. So, let's think about how you can apply this knowledge to really make a difference in your daily life.

The wisdom of youth

Remember when you were a kid and you would say, "I'm rubber, you're glue. Anything you say bounces off me and sticks to you!" We were so wise when we were children! If we could only follow the advice from our childhood now. Imagine the freedom of not allowing what others say to stick to you! Imagine not walking around all day repeating negative conversations—ruminating.

Visualize protecting yourself. Create your rubber. Imagine your force field. Most important, when someone calls you a bad name or is negative, DO NOT ENGAGE! Nonengagement is a powerful tool. Think, *I am rubber, you are glue.* You don't have to verbalize it, just think it and walk away. Nothing stops a bully more than not getting a rise out of you. Bullies are everywhere, not just at school. They are part of our families and our workplace. Usually, these people are responding just as we would expect them to. It is their typical behavior! When someone acts this way, say to yourself, "Typical of _____." Then shorten it—the initials and repetition will help! So, if your mother is just behaving in the way that your mother usually does, but it is upsetting to you, say "T.O.M, T.O.M, T.O.M. Typical of Mom!" Don't allow your mother to trigger a stressful, unhealthy reaction in your body!

Draw a colorful force field around the body. What positive words can you think about to help your field to remain strong?

Worry. What a waste of energy!

I come from a long line of worriers. I used to be one (I do my best to not be anymore). Worrying is useless and destructive to your body. You can stop it. You really can!

It goes back to the idea of awareness. Remember, you can't take care of it if you are not aware of it! The first step in stopping worry is to notice when and why you are worrying.

Draw images or write words describing your worries. Keep track for a few days.

SUN	MON	TUES	WED	THURS	FRI	SAT

Once you are aware of what you are worrying about, think about each thing. Can you fix it? Can someone fix it for you? Is this something that can be controlled?

The *only* thing that we have control over is our *own* reaction and the actions that you choose to take. Nothing else. You can't control your spouse's reaction, your boss's reaction, not even your dog's! Only your own. That's all you get. So, choose your reactions carefully.

Will you choose to worry? Will that help? If you NEED to worry and you can't let go, then allow yourself a limited amount of worry time. Go ahead, do it here, I will wait. Take five or ten minutes and write out your worries. Do the *write and rip!* exercise again. Release your worries.

Use color, line, and shape to express your worries or write them out and scribble on top of them.

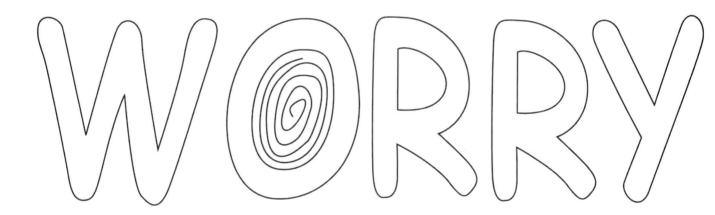

When you have finished, go do something to distract your mind! Every time that you catch yourself worrying, continue to acknowledge the worry. Question if you can do anything. Choose your reaction. Then go do something else.

Change the channel with a remote control in your brain.

You have the power to change the images in your mind. When you catch yourself worrying, imagining a negative future outcome, see that vision, click an imaginary remote control in your brain, and change the image! The next channel will have a more favorable view of the future. Every time that you imagine changing the image, you can imagine a more satisfying outcome. Don't keep replaying the same old channel over and over!

It is also helpful to use the pause button on your imaginary remote. Feeling anxious, overwhelmed, annoyed? Press pause. Stop for a moment. Freeze the picture. Look around at where you are. Describe the scene to yourself. What do you see on the screen? You are the director of this show. Slow it down—take a moment to pause before yelling "action." You have control of the remote. No one else is watching this screen. Remember to use the remote anytime that you need it.

First, draw the negative station on the screen, then click (it helps to blink your eyes!) and draw the positive outcome.

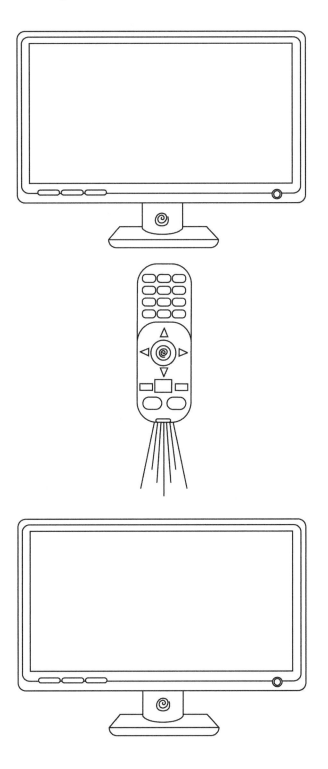

The Serenity Prayer

American theologian Reinhold Niebuhr has helped countless people throughout the world with these famous words: "God, give us grace to accept with serenity the things that cannot be changed, courage to change the things that should be changed, and the wisdom to distinguish the one from the other" (1943). Many support groups use these words to encourage participants to release their worries. It does not matter what your belief system is, it's about awareness. It is about analyzing a situation and either creating change or letting it go. Releasing the situation to the universe, to a higher power, to anything greater than yourself. What are your beliefs? Can your beliefs help you let go of a worry?

Use line, shape, and color to create an image of your higher power. You can be as abstract or realistic as you want. There is no right or wrong. Belief is based on individual thought. Include an image of yourself releasing your worry to your higher power. If creating this image is difficult for you, please seek the help of a psychological professional, member of the clergy, or spiritual leader.

Guilty as charged!

It can be difficult to release our worries. Sometimes, it is even harder to release our guilt. . . . Self-forgiveness is a human struggle. We are often harder on ourselves than on anyone else. Holding on to the past does not help your stress level in the present. It is important to find a way to forgive yourself and to forgive others. What are you holding on to? How long has it been? We are all hopefully changing and growing and learning as we age. Are you the same person that you were when this event happened? Can you forgive your younger, less wise self or the younger, less wise person who wronged you? Entire books are written on the subject of forgiveness.

There are many ways that you can express and release your guilt or blame and help you to move toward forgiveness.

Using biodegradable paper (craft paper works well, like a paper shopping bag) and a pencil, journal about the issue that you are having difficulty letting go of. Go to your favorite body of water. Running water is preferable, like a stream or river. Release your writing. Let it go. It will disintegrate. No one will know. Send the past away from you. If there is no water near you, then you can bury your writing. The rain will dissolve the paper. Rip it up first. Plant a plant over it, mix it into your compost, and allow the past to help grow something beautiful for the future.

If you are truly not ready to let go, then lock your writing up in a safe and special place. Perhaps as you grow, gain perspective, and become more wise, there will be a later time in your life when you will truly be ready to let go.

Imagine the person whom you have wronged in the past. If possible, visualize an imaginary path to wherever they are now. Can you send love to that person? Or, are you able to simply wish them well?

Find a photograph of yourself from around the time of this event. Glue or tape it here (make a photo copy first if you would like). Can you send love to your past self? Draw something joyful on or around this photo. Try to smile at your past self as you do this.

Now try to visualize an imaginary path to a person who has wronged you.

What is the purpose of feeling any connection with this person in your life now? If this is someone that you no longer need in your life, then imagine that there is a cord linking you to this person—the cord can be as long as it needs to be, it can reach another state or even country! Now take out your scissors, *cut* the cord! In your mind, cut the connection between you and this person. They can no longer reach you, they can't affect you emotionally. You are safe from their thoughts and actions. If it is difficult for you to visualize this, then draw a path on a map or create a map on paper representing the connection. Cut it up.

If the person who wronged you is still in your life, take a moment to picture them as they were in the past. Try to remember if there were good times that you experienced together. Was there laughter? Was there joy? If you have a photo of this person, repeat the above activity, try to smile at them. Can you mend this relationship? Do you want to? Can you do your best to release negative feelings toward them even if you are not able to fully forgive them at this time? Can you disconnect yourself from the emotions surrounding the circumstances? If you can't cut the cord to them, try to visualize cutting the cord to the situation and your residual feelings.

If a particular event in your life is filling your bucket and affecting your ability to release your stress then it is important that you seek the help of a psychological professional, member of the clergy or spiritual leader.

"The sun is always shining behind the clouds." (American proverb)

Prolonged stress can lead to depression. There is a great difference between depressive symptoms and diagnosable depression. If your feelings of sadness are overwhelming and preventing you from your normal daily routine, or if you feel like you may hurt yourself or someone else, please go see your primary care doctor, therapist, or psychiatrist, or go to the nearest emergency room or dial 911.

We all experience the blues now and again; it is normal and healthy. It is important to allow yourself quiet time to relax. Make sure that you balance your down time with activity time. An object in motion stays in motion, but an object at rest (for too long) gets depressed! Try to remember a period in your life when you were feeling down. Perhaps you were physically unwell. The longer you did nothing, the harder it became to get moving again. Quiet times of sedate activities are very important, but they need to be balanced with physical movement in order to keep your stress levels down. *Inactivity feeds depression.* It is easier for the black cloud to surround you when you are not moving! The couch or your bed can easily become a deep, dark hole if you lie there for too long!

What does depression look like to you? Create an abstract drawing using line, shape, and color, or draw an image of depression.

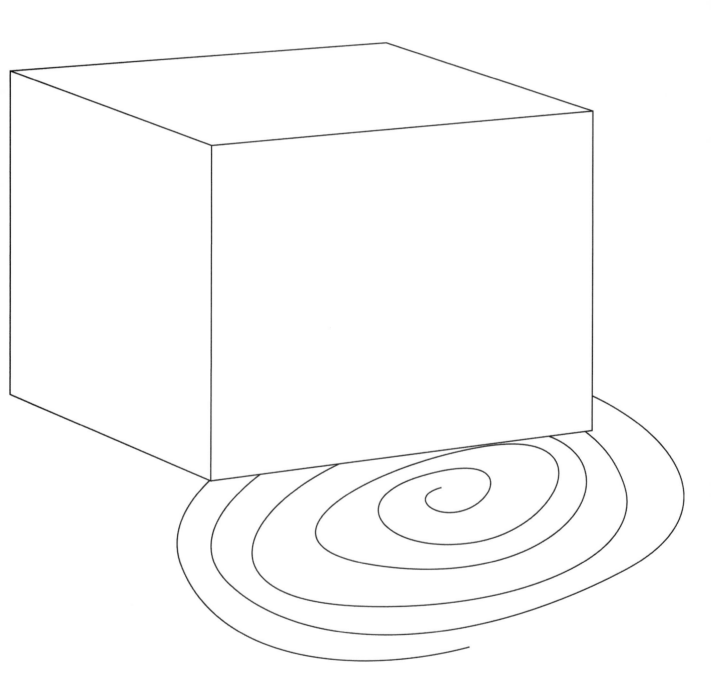

Balance your scale. Collage images of restful activities on one side of the scale and images of more physical activities on the other.

Positive ways to help yourself

You don't get it unless you got it.

Support groups can be very beneficial. Whether online or in person, it always helps to be with people who truly understand what you are going through because they are having similar experiences. There are all sorts of support groups. There are grief groups, groups for various mental health diagnosis, physical ailments, divorce, adoption, and yes—even for stress. You name it, and there's a group for that! There may not be a group near you, but there is surely an online forum. It is important to realize that everyone's situation will be different. Never follow any medical advice from a forum without consulting your physician first.

Imagine yourself being fully supported. Create an image of yourself surrounded by supportive, understanding people.

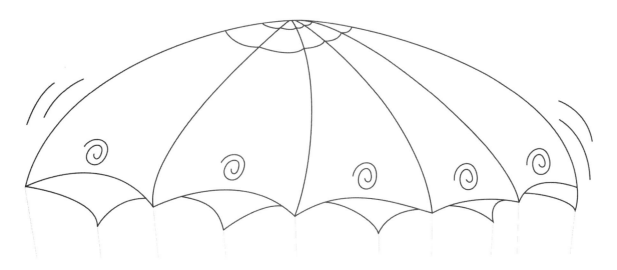

Draw or paste in a picture of yourself and your favorite support people (or animals).

Thank you!

Really think about the last image. Smile. Send these people love. Feel gratitude for them. Gratitude is an often-neglected emotion. It is incredibly important to make time in your daily routine to recognize gratitude for the people, places, and things that surround us. The sunshine, chocolate ice cream, the person who said good morning with a smile, or gave you the parking spot. Be grateful. *Feel* gratitude. Take a moment to place your hands on your heart and breathe. Be grateful that you can breathe. In your mind, take a moment to list a few things that you are grateful for.

Is your Gratitude Glass half full or half empty? Are you paying attention to filling it? Using magazines or your own photographs, fill this glass with what you are grateful for today. Write a list if you prefer. Gratitude is not just for Thanksgiving Day. We need to feel it and express it daily!

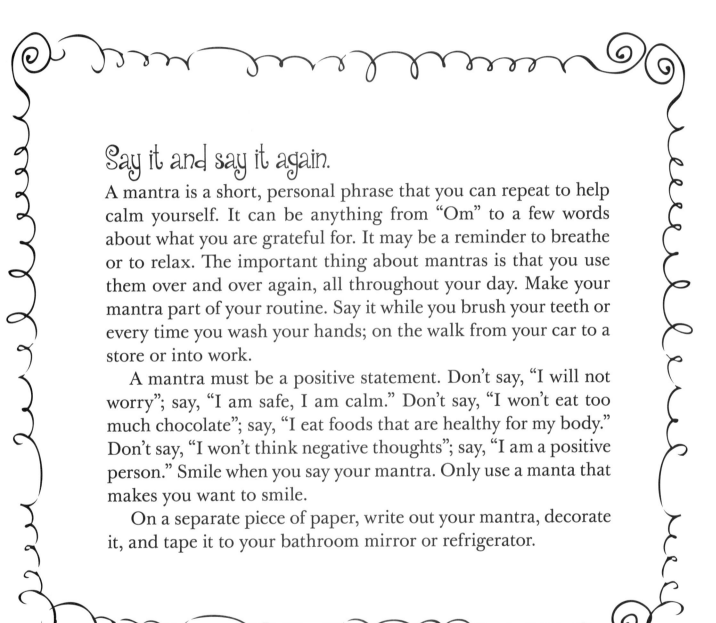

Say it and say it again.

A mantra is a short, personal phrase that you can repeat to help calm yourself. It can be anything from "Om" to a few words about what you are grateful for. It may be a reminder to breathe or to relax. The important thing about mantras is that you use them over and over again, all throughout your day. Make your mantra part of your routine. Say it while you brush your teeth or every time you wash your hands; on the walk from your car to a store or into work.

A mantra must be a positive statement. Don't say, "I will not worry"; say, "I am safe, I am calm." Don't say, "I won't eat too much chocolate"; say, "I eat foods that are healthy for my body." Don't say, "I won't think negative thoughts"; say, "I am a positive person." Smile when you say your mantra. Only use a manta that makes you want to smile.

On a separate piece of paper, write out your mantra, decorate it, and tape it to your bathroom mirror or refrigerator.

Mood Music

You can even use a favorite lyric to create your mantra: "All you need is love," "Put on a happy face," "Imagine," "Take a look at yourself and make that change," "Get up, stand up, don't give up the fight," "Don't worry, be happy . . ."

Music can be a powerful release to express and alter your mood. Blasting loud and angry music in your car and screaming at the top of your lungs can really help you to release your stress. Just make sure that the windows are closed so you don't frighten a pedestrian! Listening to your favorite upbeat song can easily lift your spirits. Singing along has the same effect as taking a moment to breathe. If you feel like you could use a good cry to release some stress, a special sad song might bring you that much-needed relief. Music has become easy to access; gone are the days of waiting for the radio disc jockey to play what we want to hear. Most people have 24-hour access to music on their cell phones. Take advantage of always having your phone with you. Download music, create song lists based on different moods. Search the Internet for spontaneous music that might help you to release and revive a mood.

Create an image representing a favorite song or lyric.

Not a singer?

Use a quote. Think of one word or words that might be helpful to you, search the Internet for quotes containing that word. There are many quote databases online. Write down your favorite quotes. Be on the lookout for words that inspire you. Purchase a quote-of-the-day calendar or sign up for free daily quote emails. Follow your favorite authors online; many send daily messages with inspirational wisdom.

Write down a list of negative thoughts. Next to each thought, write how you can twist it to be a positive mantra.

Limiting Belief   Positive Mantra

Jill Howell

Write some inspiring quotes that you love here.

You are what you eat.

Food also has a great effect on our mood. Heavy foods can either weigh you down and make you feel sluggish, or help you to feel more grounded when you are feeling flighty and all over the place. Eating light and natural foods can lessen the feelings of a heavy load. Food is comfort. Emotional attachments to food remind us of different times and people in our life. We eat every day. Have you ever noticed how crabby and more easily stressed you feel when you skip a meal? I completely stop functioning like a stove without fuel. We need food to maintain proper brain and gut function. Think about how cranky you are if you don't move your bowels regularly. Moving your bowels releases toxins, including stress!

Every day, food can serve as a source of pleasure and healing or it can send us into a whirlwind of bad memories, make us tired, and reduce our tolerance for stress. The chemicals in our food greatly affect our mood. Certain foods affect the serotonin levels in our gut and our brain. Serotonin is the hormone that helps to produce a sense of well-being. There are many books written about the specific foods needed to help with moods. Please seek advice from a doctor, nutritionist, or dietician about the ways that food can help your moods.

Color and collage the two figures. In one figure, include healthy food choices and colors that reflect how the food makes you feel. In the other, show how you feel on a bad day when you have made poor food choices (don't be hard on yourself, we all have days like that!).

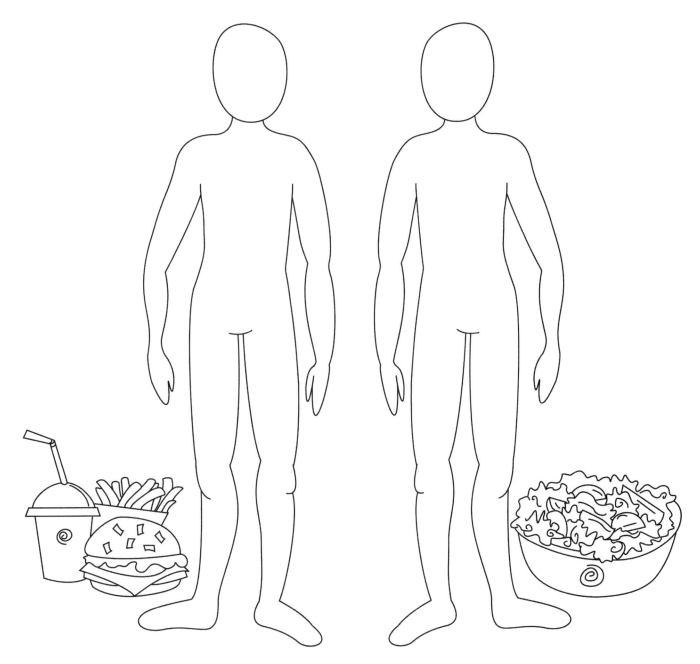

Forty minutes of bliss!

That's how long it takes to escape into a recording of a one-hour show without the commercials. On weekdays, I look forward to sitting down when the day is done and pressing *play* on my favorite soap opera! I retreat from my world and escape into theirs. It's a great time to check out, or to check in with emails and Facebook, and surf the Internet, as I watch their lives go by on the screen. These are their problems, far-fetched and unrealistic (and really fun to watch). Escaping into someone else's fictional life for a moment is a healthy distraction. You can't possibly focus on your own troubles when you are waiting for the results of your favorite character's paternity test, or not knowing who survived the explosion from last week's cliff-hanger.

Find a show that you love. Something that really interests you, reality-based or fiction. Something that can draw you in. That you would be willing to watch a marathon of, if you only had the time. Something that promotes daydreaming. How would you decorate that island getaway home? Would you love it or list it? Imagine yourself on that stage singing in front of those judges, dancing with those stars. Could you really eat those disgusting bugs?

Television can be fun, in moderation. Movies can be even better. Television has commercial breaks; even if you are fast-forwarding through the commercials, your mind is still pausing from the story and providing an opportunity for your brain to focus on personal concerns. When you watch a two-hour movie without any distractions, it really gives your mind and body a chance to rest. Unless, of course, you are watching an edge-of-your-seat action adventure or thriller. These movies do create a stress reaction in your body; it is not a prolonged reaction, however, and since the adventure is not your own, your body will quickly be able to calm itself.

Sad movies are an excellent way to release pent-up emotions.

Sometimes we feel like crying, but we just can't. Watch something sad, even a sappy television commercial, and *boom*, instant release. Keep a few favorites on hand, movies that you already know the ending to in case you really need to sob through it. Who can survive watching *The Notebook*, *Beaches*, or even *Toy Story 3* without going through a box of tissues? *Schindler's List* will certainly help to put your life in perspective.

You've heard the saying "laughter is the best medicine." Even just smiling can make us feel better. Smile now, go ahead, you can do it. Even when we don't feel like it, smiling can help change our mood. Smiling helps to reduce stress by triggering happy brain chemicals (endorphins) to counteract the stressful ones (cortisol). Laughter can temporarily release all feelings of stress from your body. When your body releases endorphins, it creates an overall sense of well-being and relaxation. It is difficult to feel grumpy while sharing a funny story or watching a funny movie. I dare you to watch *Young Franken-stein*, *Airplane*, or *Caddyshack* without giggling, despite whatever mood you were in when you pressed *play*.

Movies are great, but books are the best. When we read a book, we activate our brains' imagining the characters and the scenes (they never look right in the movie version!). A good book can take you away for hours at a time or you can take a month reading for a few minutes at a time. Each time, your brain will go right back to instantly imagining foreign lands and adventures.

Do you have a long commute? Even a twenty-minute commute can be made less stressful by listening to an audiobook. Instead of spending your commute focusing on everything that you need to do today and everything that may have gone wrong, get absorbed in someone else's story. Listen to your favorite novels, or inspirational or humorous talk shows and interviews.

Take some time to think about the books, movies, and television shows in your life that have really had an effect on you. What are your go-to favorites?

List your favorites in each section, then use color to highlight which ones help you to cry, to feel inspired, to release anger, or provide a joyful escape. Decide for yourself which color best represents the emotion.

Now do the same thing for all of the unread books that are piling up on your shelf, and the long list of unwatched shows and movies that are recorded on your television . . . which ones would you most want to watch or read if you would only make the time?

Warning: Too much reality may be hazardous to your health!

Make careful choices when deciding what to watch on television and in the movies. The images we see get planted into our brains; what you choose to watch may return to you in your dreams. Disturbing images from the news and the realism we watch in dramatic television shows and movies are sorted through our minds and filed away in the brain just like our personal experiences.

The news can be shocking, dramatic, and just sad. When we hear about devastation all around the planet that is out of our control, it can be very difficult to process. Sometimes during a major news event, we glue ourselves to the television or the Internet watching the same images over and over. This is not helping your stress level. Watch it once and then turn it off.

A place for everything and everything in its place!

Difficulty focusing is a sure sign of stress. When our minds are cluttered with thoughts, having clutter surround us only makes it more difficult to focus. Look around you now: are you reading this book in a space that promotes relaxation, or are you looking at piles of things that need to be taken care of? Stacks of unread magazines, mail that needs to be sorted, laundry to be put away. Clutter controls our brains, inside and out. We have too many thoughts and too much stuff!

One of the biggest causes of clutter is that most people buy too much. Who can resist a great bargain? It's hard to drive past the garage sale without stopping or not sneak a peek at the 70%-off sale! Remember your bucket and the concept of awareness. We need to become more aware of what we are purchasing. To think twice, even three times before we bring more items into our houses, our closets, and our brains.

I love a good purge. It feels wonderful to lighten our loads and pass things that we are not using on to others. There are many books, blogs, and articles about how and what to purge. Decluttering is a big industry. You can even hire someone to help you sort through all of your stuff. A professional can also help you decide which items to sell and which to donate. There are many charities that will accept gently used goods and clothing. It feels great to know that someone else is making use of your stuff, and it's much better for the environment than throwing things away.

Begin by creating an image of the place in your house that is your greatest clutter problem area. Mine is my kitchen counter. Everyone drops everything there. It is the first place that we see when we walk in the door, so it is an easy drop-off spot. However, since it is the where we enter our home, the mess is the first thing we see when we get home. This does not help to create a stress-free home. It makes you feel like you always have to clean up.

Collage or draw a cluttered space in your life.

When you have completed the image, look through some magazines and create a collage with a few images of similar spaces reorganized. Spaces with nice baskets or shelving, or that just appeal to you as a space that you would like to be in.

What are you waiting for?

The fabulous party dress that sits with its tags on in your closet is calling you, "Wear me! You looked and felt so pretty when you tried me on!" We all have things in our home that we are saving for a special occasion. Make today the special occasion. Make every day special. What are you truly waiting for? Of course you are not going to open a bottle of champagne every day, but certainly at a gathering with friends or family, you can find something worthy of a toast. How about your grandmother's china sitting on display, gathering dust? Surely the meal that you took the time and care to prepare deserves to be placed on something special.

Why are you waiting? Do you believe that you don't deserve to use these things? If that is the case, try just doing it. Use an item, wear the dress, and see how it makes you feel. Are you able to allow yourself these small moments of pleasure—can you indulge a whim? It's healthy to spoil yourself once in a while. If you use the special things every day, then they will lose their personal value, but enjoying and sharing your treasures will help you to value them more.

Fill this closet with items that you consider only for special occasions.

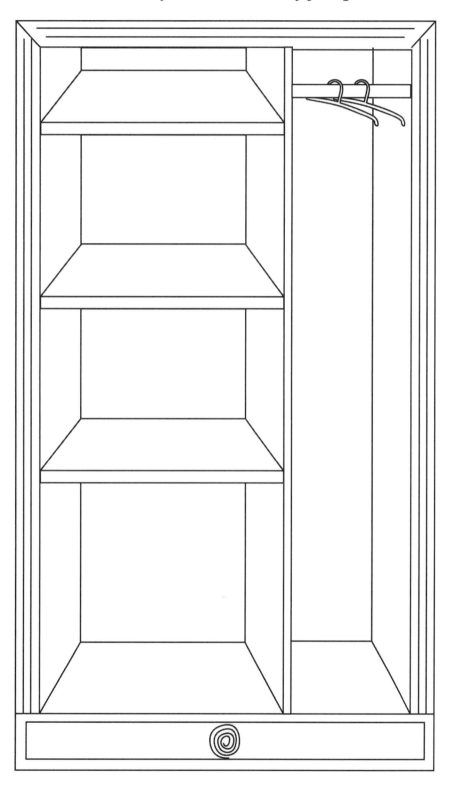

Use line, color, and shape to express the joy that you may feel using some of these things more often. Or draw yourself twirling in your party dress!

Stuck in your own web

Too many thoughts and too many things. Too much to do and too much stuff. Spinning and spinning the web in your brain. The thoughts get stuck, with no way to release them from the sticky web that you have created in your mind. Stop in this moment and become aware of all of the thoughts that are sticking to your mind.

Write, draw, or collage images on the web to represent the thoughts that you are stuck on.

Recharging your inner battery

It is important to identify the activities and the people that drain or fuel our battery packs. Some people completely exhaust us, while others will leave us feeling rejuvenated and energized. Activities have the same power. Of course, there are many activities or chores that we must do whether they tire or revive us. It's hard to make scooping the kitty litter fun no matter how you look at it!

Remember, all you are in control of is your own attitude! Check in with yourself. Do you allow tasks to drain you? Can you complete a task without complaining, even to yourself? Focus more on the enjoyable tasks, squeeze more energy out of them so you will feel less drained by the thankless tasks.

Take some time to identify which activities drain you and which fuel you. Collage, draw, or write inside the batteries. Are they equal? Are there many more draining activities than fueling ones? Can you make the draining activities only use small AAA-size amounts of energy and the reviving ones use the large D-cell amount of your fuel? It's all in how you twist your attitude toward what you are doing.

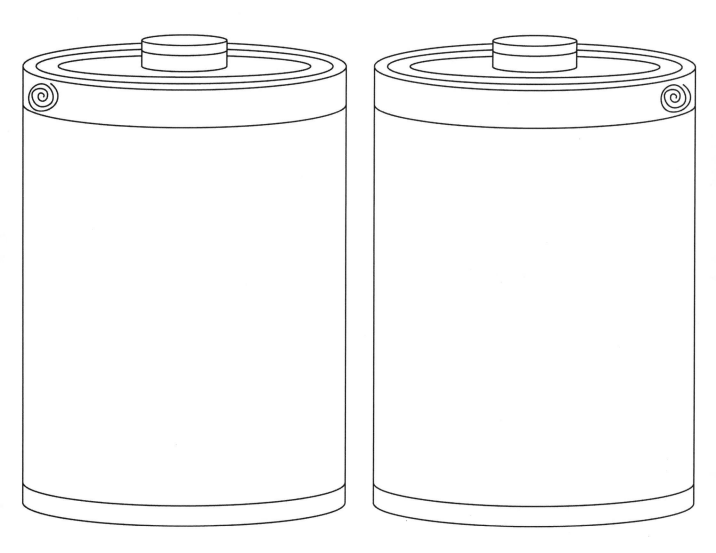

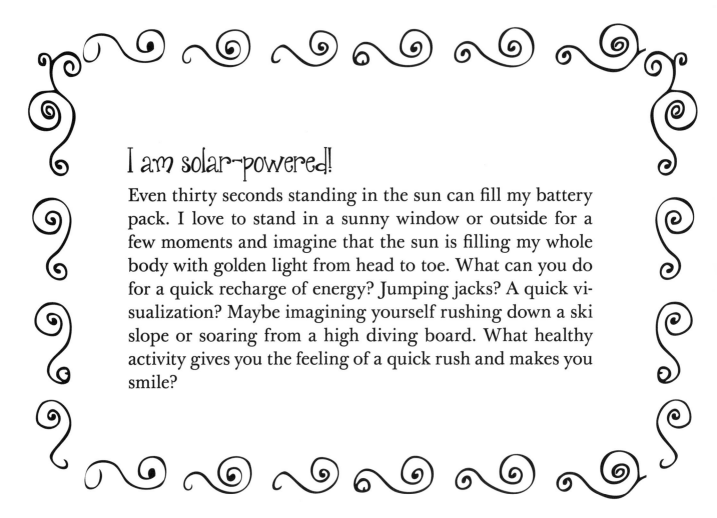

I am solar-powered!

Even thirty seconds standing in the sun can fill my battery pack. I love to stand in a sunny window or outside for a few moments and imagine that the sun is filling my whole body with golden light from head to toe. What can you do for a quick recharge of energy? Jumping jacks? A quick visualization? Maybe imagining yourself rushing down a ski slope or soaring from a high diving board. What healthy activity gives you the feeling of a quick rush and makes you smile?

So much to do, so little time.

So let's do it all at once! Does multitasking really work? No, not really. It definitely doesn't save time. It takes more concentration for the brain to switch back and forth between thoughts or activities than it does to remain mindful and complete one task at a time. When we multitask, our brains don't fully engage in the activities at hand. If we do a single task, it gives the brain a chance to mindfully rest on one thing. This allows the brain to get into the zone, to focus, to allow for creative flow. When we are mindful, we can do a better job at the task at hand.

Think about how much you are missing when you are on your phone. Walking and talking, driving and talking, exercising and talking, or even worse, texting. These are all missed opportunities to allow the mind to de-stress. Will you stop and smell the roses during your walk if you are in the middle of an intense conversation? Connecting with nature even for a moment can release tension. Obviously, if you get into an automobile accident because you were focused on a conversation instead of the road, your life will be much more stressful!

Do one thing at a time. Try it—try just eating. Mindfully. Paying attention to your food, the tastes, the textures. You will eat less than if you gobble down your food while watching television or flipping through a magazine.

Be with the person you are with. Truly pay attention to them. Put your phone away and have a conversation. Connecting with others reduces our stress. Stopping midconversation to read a text from someone else is not only rude, it affects our relationships. It is important to look at others while we converse, to read their faces, to react and show them that we care. This builds stronger relationships.

Try to be mindful about the simple tasks that need to be done. When you wash the dishes or fold your clothes, just do the task at hand. Focus on the bubbles, on folding neat edges. You will do the task better, and you will give your mind a rest from the mental clutter.

Color this mandala and label it with simple tasks and chores that you can try to do more mindfully.

Fido and Fluffy

Our pets provide us with a wonderful opportunity to slow down and destress. They are great teachers of being in the here and now. Take the time to really watch your pets. Watch them as they curl up in a sunny spot or on your lap demanding instant love and affection. Watch as they stretch every time they rise. Observe the pure joy when they run and play. Animals have an amazing appreciation for nature. They revel in the joy of rolling in the grass (or in something stinky), running through water, climbing up hills. There is so much to be learned from animals. If you don't have a pet, then watching videos of animals doing funny things is always a great way to lighten a bad mood. Who can hold back a smile when they see a kitten try to jump too high and fall over or get stuck inside a box?

Take the time to be with and appreciate your pets, even if only for a random moment. Draw or collage an image of your pet or pets or an image of an animal that you think that you would love to have as a pet.

Weed your garden.

Some people fertilize us and help us grow, while others are weeds that hold us back and choke our ideas. Just as it is important in your garden to know the difference between the flowers, the plants, and the weeds, it is important to recognize the nurturing people in our life. Really think about your most important influences. Think about your relationships, your friendships, even your coworkers and acquaintances. Even casual relationships can drain your energy. Our time is limited; don't waste your energy constantly pulling out weeds. Focus on nurturing the flowers, growing the relationships that are positive and healthy. Pull the weeds out and let them go.

Color the garden, label the flowers with the names of nurturing people in your life or the ones who help you to stay rooted. Now label the weeds— trust yourself, you know who they are. No one has to see this. Use initials or nicknames if that helps you to feel more comfortable.

He did it!

If you grew up with siblings or cousins, you're all too familiar with both sides of "It wasn't me, Mom, he did it!" We have all been blamed for something that we didn't do, and we have all been the blame-thrower. It's really easy to not accept responsibility for our actions. There is always an easy scapegoat to pin the blame on. Blaming others can cause you more stress. Certainly the accused party will become rightly defensive. You may also feel guilt for the false accusation. It's always better in the long run to accept the responsibility if you have done something wrong. It is better for your self-respect, and others will respect you owning up to your wrongdoings. It may be more stressful in the moment, but if you deal with your mistakes right away, then they are not able to grow into even bigger problems.

Fill the image with words of blame describing who you are blaming and what you are blaming them for.

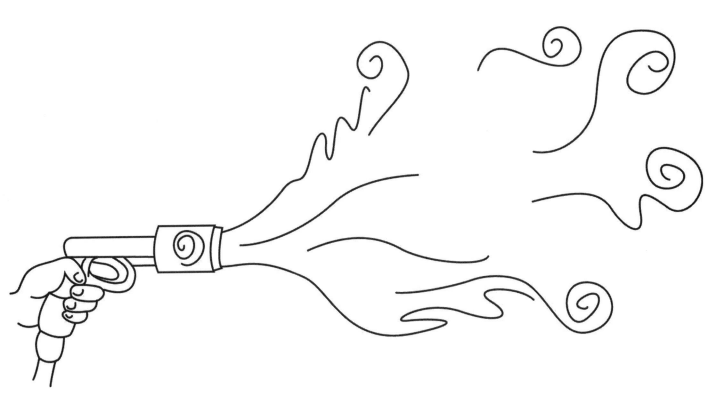

Gain some perspective.

Other people have shoes that hurt, too. There are many sayings about walking a mile in another person's shoes. It is important to try to understand how others are feeling. To imagine what it feels like to be them. To imagine how they are viewing us. Try to step outside of yourself for a few moments. Is there someone in your life who is difficult to deal with? Try to imagine how their day is going. Take some time to visualize waking up as them. Could there be stressors in their life that you don't know about? Maybe that nasty coworker is exhausted from taking care of a sick family member. Perhaps the person who cut you off driving to work this morning really was having an emergency. We truly don't know what another person is feeling until we walk in their shoes for a day.

Color these shoes and label the ones that remind you of someone in your life.

Volunteering: It's not all about you (well actually, it is)!

Helping others is a great way to help yourself. When we contribute to the well-being of others, it helps us to feel a sense of pride, self-worth, and accomplishment. Sometimes when we are feeling too much stress, we isolate ourselves. Having a commitment to volunteer somewhere can help to break the funk and help us to gain perspective. Listening to other people's problems helps us to separate from our own difficulties, at least for the moment. Empathizing with someone else's concerns and unfortunate circumstances can help you to see your own situation more clearly.

The Corporation for National & Community Service (www.volunteeringinamerica.gov) conducted research on the benefits of volunteering. Through a compilation of various studies, they found that even when controlling for other factors such as age, health, and gender, when individuals volunteer for a minimum of one to two hours per week, they are more likely to live longer and feel happier.

What have you done for someone else today?

You may not be able to fit volunteering into your already-filled schedule, but how about random acts of kindness? Take a moment to smile at someone, to say good morning, to open a door. Help someone to reach for something at a store, carry someone's bag (ask permission first!), pay for someone's cup of coffee. These small acts can help you to step out of your own bad mood, they can break the moment, and the negative thought cycle. When someone is smiling at you with gratitude, it is an opportunity to connect with each other and to step away from yourself.

Random acts of kindness.

Can you remember a time when someone did something nice for you that was totally unexpected? How did it make you feel? How would you feel if you could make someone else feel that way? It can feel great to lighten someone else's load or help to release their stress.

Look through magazines for ideas about where you can volunteer, and create a collage of possibilities. Then contact your library, religious affiliation, or other civic organization to get involved with your community.

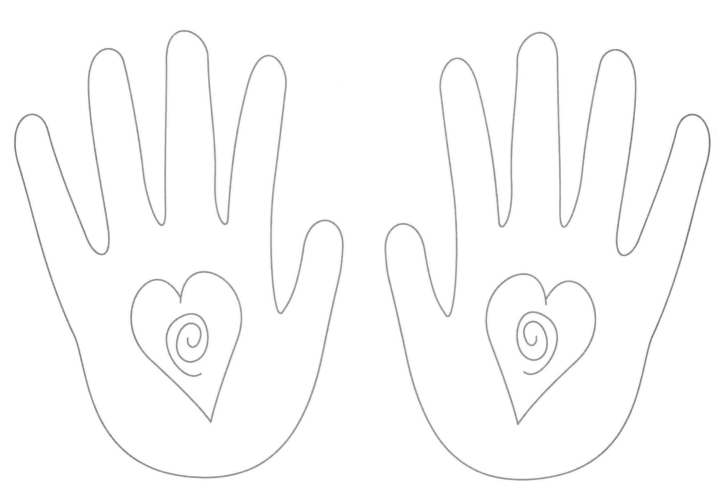

Draw a picture or collage an image that reminds you of a time when someone did something nice for you.

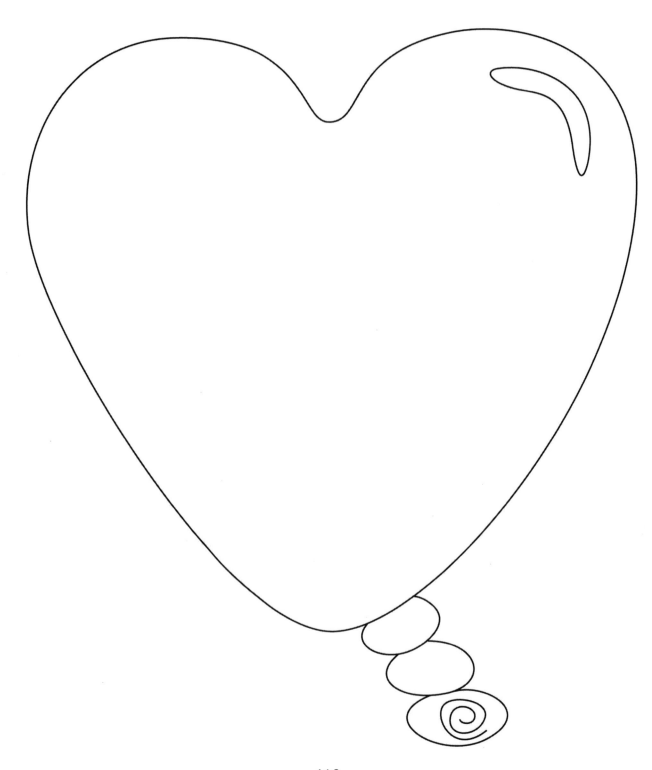

Draw a picture of a random act of kindness that you would appreciate someone doing for you. Would you be able to do that or something similar for someone else? Give it a try as soon as the opportunity presents itself. If you are not ready, then start by paying attention to potential opportunities and ideas.

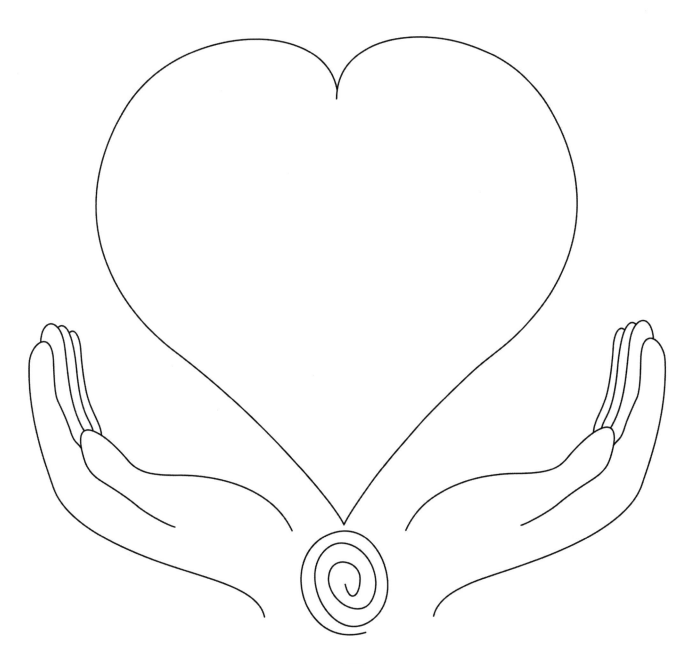

Five years from now

When we are in the midst of experiencing a stressful event in our lives, it sometimes feels like we will never make it through. There is a lot that can be learned from your past experiences. You did survive. You may even be a stronger person because of it. Believe it or not, you may even feel grateful for the difficult times because they have helped you to become the person that you are today.

Think about some of the major stressful events that have happened in your life. When you look back at them, what have you learned? What got you through them? Who helped you? How did you grow? Do they seem as important five years later? Ten years later?

Now think about the stressors in your life now. How will they look in five years? Ten? What have you learned to help you through them now?

Label the top of the hourglass with some of your stressful life events. As they squeeze through time, how do they look on the bottom? Are they smaller? Less colorful?

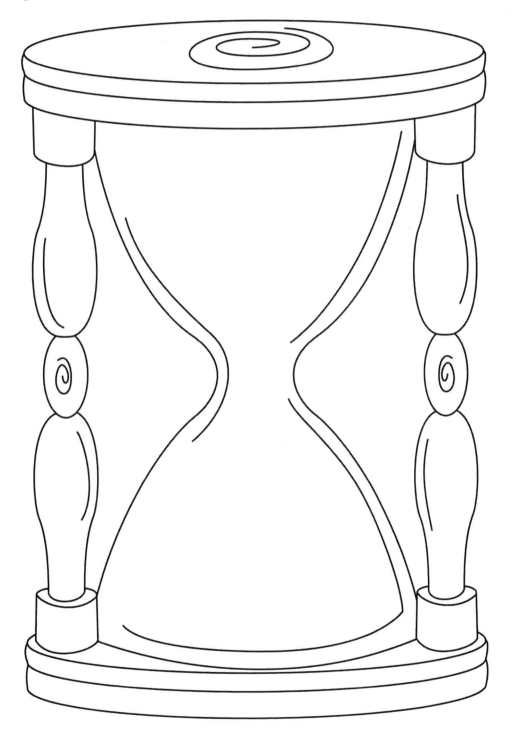

Every day is a fresh start.

Every morning when you open your eyes, you can decide to be more mindful. Every morning you can choose to focus on your breath. To pause for a moment. To take some time for yourself today. To play a game, work on a hobby, exercise, sing. Each day is a new day. If yesterday didn't go so well, that is okay—brush it off, start again today. Make better choices today. Consult with a counselor or clergy to help guide you if it is difficult for you to make changes on your own. Check in with your bucket, your stress level, and use intention to create a plan of self-care.

Create an image of intention based on what you have learned in this workbook. What will you do differently? What changes have you already made? What will your life look like when you have made some changes? Go ahead— color, draw, and collage your way to a less stressful life!

Acknowledgments

I would like to thank my editor Leah Zarra, and the team at Skyhorse Publishing for recognizing this book's potential to help people. Thank you, Leah, for your support and your patience with my many, many questions.

Thank you to my parents for raising me to believe that I can do anything I set my mind to. You have always been my best cheerleaders.

To my helpers: thank you, Michelle M., for proving that distance and time don't affect true friendship. Ilene B., you are my ethical compass. Peggy K., you keep me goal-oriented and safe. Evelyn S., you are my sanity keeper. Sandy M.C., you are a living example of grace under pressure and a constant reminder to keep my heart open.

To my mentors: Joanne O., you keep my energy flowing and my life grounded. Lynn S., you lead by example, teaching me to be still, to witness, and to accept.

Thank you to my immediate and extended families, and many dear friends for your constant love and support.

To Rob, you are my heart's song. You are my voice. You are my rock. You are my home.

Kagan, you are my spirit. I hope to teach you that you, too, can do anything you set your mind to.

Please join my community!
Go To
facebook.com/Color-Draw-Collage-Create-Your-Way-to-a-Less-Stress-ful-Life-1099855170097634/
and post your images from the workbook or comments and questions.
Thanks!
Jill